Hedia Zardi

BEEDEA's Performance on Knapsack problem

Hédia Zardi

BEEDEA's Performance on Knapsack problem

Study of the performance of the Balanced Explore Exploit Distributed Evolutionary Algorithm "BEEDEA" on the multiobjective knapsack problem

Éditions universitaires européennes

Imprint
Any brand names and product names mentioned in this book are subject to trademark, brand or patent protection and are trademarks or registered trademarks of their respective holders. The use of brand names, product names, common names, trade names, product descriptions etc. even without a particular marking in this work is in no way to be construed to mean that such names may be regarded as unrestricted in respect of trademark and brand protection legislation and could thus be used by anyone.

Cover image: www.ingimage.com

Publisher:
Éditions universitaires européennes
is a trademark of
International Book Market Service Ltd., member of OmniScriptum Publishing Group
17 Meldrum Street, Beau Bassin 71504, Mauritius

Printed at: see last page
ISBN: 978-613-1-57616-4

Ministry of the Higher Education, Scientific Research and Technology

University of Monastir

*_*_*_*_*

High School of Computer Science and Mathematics of Monastir

Final project report

To obtain the

Diploma of Bachelor degree in Computer Science

Study of the performance of

the Balanced Explore Exploit Distributed Evolutionary Algorithm

"BEEDEA"

on the multiobjective knapsack problem

Realized by

ZARDI HEDIA

Directed by

Mme GZARA MARIEM

Academic year: 2008/2009

Dedication

Special dedication to my dears: my father Sadok, my dear mother Samira, my sisters Nagiba, Dorra and Yorsa and to my lovely brothers Rachid and Salim for the help and the encouragement,

and for all the member of my family.

--*I really love you*-*-*

Very special dedication for my best friends

ZARDI HEDIA

Thanks

Before starting my report, I would like to direct

all my thoughts of gratitude toward Mme Gzara Mariem to have wanted to

supervise my project, for her help and her precious information.

Then, I take advantage of this opportunity

to express my recognition to all our teachers in ISIMM,

and all person who contributed to the realization of my project.

ZARDI HEDIA

Abstract

Most real world problems require the simultaneous optimization of multiple, competing, criteria (or objectives). In this case, the aim of a multi-objective resolution approach is to find a number of solutions known as Pareto-optimal solutions. Evolutionary algorithms manipulate a population of solutions and thus are suitable to solve multi-objective optimization problems. In addition parallel evolutionary algorithms aim at reducing the computation time and solving large combinatorial optimization problems. In this work we study the performance of the "Balanced Explore Exploit Distributed Evolutionary Algorithm" (BEEDEA) [1] on the multi-objective Knapsack problem which is a combinatorial optimization problem. BEEDA is implemented after some improvements and tested on the Knapsack problem.

Key words: multi-objective optimization, evolutionary algorithms, Knapsack problem, distributed metaheuristics.

Résumé

La majorité des problèmes d'optimisation réels nécessitent l'optimisation simultanée de plusieurs critères (objectifs) qui sont souvent conflictuels. Dans ce cas, le but d'une approche de résolution multiobjectif est de chercher à déterminer tout un ensemble de solutions connues comme étant solutions Pareto optimales. Les algorithmes évolutionnaires, qui manipulent une population de solutions, sont donc bien adaptés à la résolution des problèmes d'optimisation multiobjectif. En plus les algorithmes évolutionnaires parallèles ont pour but de réduire le temps d'exécution et de résoudre des problèmes d'optimisation de très grande taille. Dans ce travail, nous avons étudié la performance de l'algorithme BEEDEA "Balanced Explore Exploit Distributed Evolutionary Algorithm" (BEEDEA) [1] sur le problème de sac à dos multi objectif. Nous avons implémenté BEEDEA après quelques améliorations et nous l'avons testé sur ce problème.

***Mots clés:** optimisation multiobjectif, algorithmes évolutionnaires, problème de sac à dos, métaheuristiques distribuées.*

Table of contents

List of figures

List of tables

List of annexes

Introduction

Evolutionary Algorithms (EAs) are efficient heuristic search methods based on Darwin evolution with powerful characteristics of robustness and flexibility to capture global solutions of complex optimization problems. Using EAs the probability of finding a near optimum solution in an early stage of the optimization process is very high. EAs have the ability to escape from local minima where deterministic optimization methods may fail or are not applicable.

EAs are easy to process in parallel. They are population-based search methods. Despite their operational simplicity, Parallel Evolutionary Algorithms (PEAs) are complex non-linear algorithms with many control parameters affecting both the quality of the search process and their efficiency.

In this work, we study the *" Balanced Explore Exploit Distributed Evolutionary Algorithm" proposed by Essabri.A [1]* .This algorithm is improved by using SPEA2 rather than SPEA as basic EAs and then evaluated on the multiobjective knapsack problem.

In the first chapter we present the basic concepts of multi-objective optimization. In the second chapter we describe the main mechanisms of evolutionary algorithms and some well known multiobjective EAs. In the third part we describe the BEEDEA algorithm and our proposed improvements. Experimental results are presented and analyzed for the multiobjective 0/1-knapsack problem. Finally conclusions are highlighted.

Chapter 1

Multi-objective Optimization

I.   *Introduction*

Most real world problems require the simultaneous optimization of multiple, often competing, criteria (or objectives), the solution to such problems is usually computed by combining them into a single criterion to be optimized, according to some utility function.

In many cases, however, the utility function is not well known a priori to the optimization process. The whole problem should then be treated as a multi-objective optimization problem with non-commensurable objectives. In this way, a number of solutions can be found (unlike single objective optimization, the solution to this problem is not a single point, but a family of points known as the Pareto-optimal set).

In this chapter we give the definition of a multi-objective optimization problem and other related concepts like Pareto dominance, Pareto optimal set and performance metrics.

II.   *Optimization problem*

An optimization problem can be represented in the following way:

Given a function $f\colon A \to \mathbf{R}$ from some set A to the real numbers, the optimization problem seeks for an element x_0 in A such that

$$f(x_0) \leq f(x) \quad \forall\, x \in A \ \ (\text{"minimization"}) \quad (1)$$

or such that

$$f(x_0) \geq f(x) \quad \forall\, x \in A \ \ (\text{"maximization"}) \quad (2)$$

Such a formulation is called an *optimization problem* or a *mathematical programming problem.* Many real-world and theoretical problems may be modeled in this general framework. Typically, A is some subset of the Euclidean space $\mathbf{R}^n$, often specified by a set of *constraints,* equalities or inequalities that the members of A have to satisfy. The domain A of f is called the **search space**, while the elements of A are called *candidate solutions* or *feasible solutions [16].*The function f is called, variously, an *objective function, cost function or energy function.* A feasible solution that minimizes (or maximizes, if that is the goal) the objective function is called an **optimal solution**.

Generally, when the feasible region or the objective function of the problem does not present convexity, there may be several local minima and maxima (figure 1), where a *local minimum* x^* is defined as a point for which there exists some $\delta > 0$ so that for all x such that

$$\|x - x^*\| \leq \delta$$

We have $\qquad\qquad f(x^*) \leq f(x) \qquad\qquad$ (3)

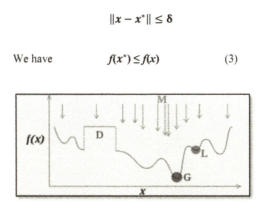

Figure 1 local minimum and global minimum

That is to say, on some region around x^* all of the function values are greater than or equal to the value at that point. Local maxima are defined similarly.

III.   *Multi-objective optimization*

A Multi-objective Optimization Problem (MOP) is defined by a quadruplet (X, D, C, f) such that:

-X is a vector of m decision variables, i.e., X = $(x_1 . . . x_m)$;

- D is a vector of m value sets defining the domains of the decision variables,

i.e., D = $(d_1 . . . d_m$);

-C is a set of constraints on X, i.e., a set of relations restricting the values that may be simultaneously assigned to the decision variables;

-and f is a vector of n>= 2 objective functions $f(x) = (f_1(x), f_2(x), ..., f_n(x))$.

There are two standard methods for treating multi-objective optimization problems:

- if a traditional optimization algorithm which minimizes a single objective is to be employed, a composite objective is constructed as follow :

$$\text{Min/Max } \bar{f} = \sum_{i=1}^{n} a_i f_i \qquad (4)$$

$$\text{Where } a_i \in [0,1] and \sum_{i=1}^{n} a_i = 1$$

- A general multi-objective optimization problem can be described as a vector function that maps a set of **m** parameters (decision variables) to a set of **n** objectives. Formally:

$$\text{Min/Max } y = f(x) = (f_1(x), f_2(x), ..., f_n(x))$$

$$\text{Subject to } x = (x_1, x_2 . . . , x_m) \in X$$

$$Y = (y_1, y_2, . . . , y_n) \in Y \qquad (5)$$

where x is called the *decision vector*, X is the *parameter space*, y is the *objective vector*, and Y is the *objective space [17]*.

14

The set of solutions of a multi-objective optimization problem in this case consists of all decision vectors for which the corresponding objective vectors cannot be improved in any dimension without degradation in another.

IV. *Pareto Dominance*

In multi-objective optimization (MO), a solution (defined by the corresponding decision vector) can be better, worse, equal, but also indifferent to another solution with respect to the objective values. "Better" means a solution is not worse in any objective and at least better in one objective than another; the superior solution is also said to *dominate* the inferior one; two solutions are "incomparable" or "indifferent" if the first one is better in one objective, the second will be better in at least one other objective.

In the case of minimization problem,

A vector $\vec{u} = (u_1, \ldots, u_n)$ is said to dominate $\vec{v} = (v_1, \ldots, v_n)$

(denoted by vector $\vec{u} \leq \vec{v}$)) if and only if **u** is partially less than **v**, i.e.,

$$\forall\, i \in \{1, \ldots, n\},\ u_i \leq v_i \ \wedge\ \exists\, i \in \{1, \ldots, n\} :\ u_i < v_i. \qquad (6)$$

V. *Pareto Optimality*

Using this concept one can define what an optimal solution is. It is a solution which is not dominated by any other solution in the search space [11]. We say that a vector of decision variables $\overrightarrow{x*} \in f$ is Pareto optimal if there does not exist another $\vec{x} \in f$ such that

$$f_i(\vec{x}) \leq f_i(\overrightarrow{x*}) \quad \forall\, i = 1, \ldots, k$$

And $f_j(\vec{x}) < f_j(\overrightarrow{x*})$ for at least one j. $\qquad (7)$

Here, f denotes the feasible region of the problem (i.e., where the constraints are satisfied).

In other words, this definition says that $\overrightarrow{x*}$ is Pareto optimal if there exist no feasible vector of decision variables $\vec{x} \in f$ which would decrease some criterion without causing a simultaneous increase in at least one other criterion. The vector $\overrightarrow{x*}$ is called non-dominated.

VI. *Pareto Optimal Set and Pareto front*

All Pareto optimal solutions form the Pareto optimal set and the plot of the objective functions whose non-dominated vectors are in the Pareto optimal set is called the Pareto front (figure 2).

For a given multi-objective optimization problem $\overrightarrow{f(x)}$, the Pareto optimal set (P*) is defined as [11]:

$$P^* := \{x \in f \mid \nexists \acute{x} \in f : \overrightarrow{f(\acute{x})} \leq \overrightarrow{f(x)} \} \qquad (8)$$

The Pareto front (PF*) is defined as:

$$PF^* := \{\vec{u} = \vec{f} = (f_1(x), \dots, f_n(x)) \mid x \in P^*\}. \qquad (9)$$

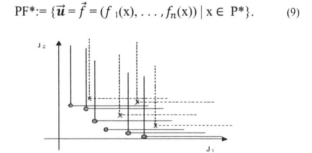

Figure 2   Illustration of the concept of Pareto front.

The Pareto Front (PF) is quite important notion in the multi-objective optimization, because all the points in this front constitute the set of solutions to the given problem. The decision maker has to select one of theses points, as an answer to his problem.

VII. *Metrics of Performance*

Comparing different optimization techniques experimentally always involves the notion of performance. In the case of multi-objective optimization, the definition of quality is substantially more complex than for single-objective optimization problems, because the optimization goal itself consists of multiple objectives:

✓ The distance of the resulting non-dominated set to the Pareto-optimal front should be minimized.

✓ A good (in most cases uniform) distribution of the solutions found is desirable [12].

Many performance criteria are proposed. We present here some of them (see annex A for more details).

- **The contribution [18]:** The contribution (Ratio of Non Dominated Individuals) measure is obtained by comparing two sets of non-dominated individuals PO1 and PO2. At first, PO2 and PO1 are mixed then the contribution of the set PO1 is determined as the ratio of the number of non-dominated solutions in PO1 which are still non-dominated in the union of PO1 and PO2 by the total number of the solutions.

- **Entropy [19]:** The entropy metric quantifies the goodness of a set of solutions in terms of distribution quality over the Pareto frontier. The higher the entropy is, the more diversified the non-dominated solutions are.

- **Generational distance [20]:** This metric calculates the average distance of the set of non-dominated solutions generated by the optimization algorithm to the true Pareto front.

- **The spacing metric:** The spacing metric gives a good indication of how evenly the solutions are distributed in the objective space.

- **Coverage [21]:** Using metric C two sets of non-dominated solutions can be compared to each other. Let A and B be two Pareto front, C(A,B) is equal to the number of solutions in B dominated by at least one solution in A divided by the total number of solutions in B.

- **Size of the dominated space [21]**: The S metric measures how much the objective space is dominated by a given non-dominated set A.

VIII.   Conclusion

An important task in multi-objective optimization is to find Pareto-optimal solutions. Their knowledge allows a decision maker to learn more about the trade-offs among the different objectives. From both a practical as well as a theoretical point of view it is desirable to have a method that is in principle able to generate all Pareto-optimal objective vectors. Evolutionary algorithms seem so suitable to solve multi-objective optimization problems. How these algorithms are able to approximate efficiently the Pareto-optimal objective vectors is the subject of the next part.

Chapter 2

Multi-Objective Evolutionary

Algorithms

I.   Introduction

Evolutionary Algorithms (EAs) are biologically-inspired optimization algorithms, imitating the process of natural evolution, and are becoming important optimization tools for several real-world applications. In this part, we describe the main concepts of EAs then some well known multiobjective EAs are presented.

II.   Genetic algorithms

Inspired by Darwin's theory of evolution in the mid 1800s, Genetic Algorithms (GAs) are computer programs which create an environment where populations of data can compete and only the fittest survive. Gas are one of the best ways to solve a problem for which little knowledge is known. They are a very general algorithm and so will work well in any search space [14].

II.1 Basics of Genetic Algorithms

The most common type of GAs works like this: a population is created with a group of individuals created randomly. The individuals in the population are then evaluated. The evaluation function is provided by the programmer and gives the individuals a score based on how well they perform at the given task. Two individuals are then selected based on their fitness. These individuals then "reproduce" to create one or more offspring, after which the offspring are mutated randomly. This continues until a suitable solution has been found or a certain

number of generations have passed, depending on the needs of the programmer
[6].The cycle of a GAs is presented in figure 3.

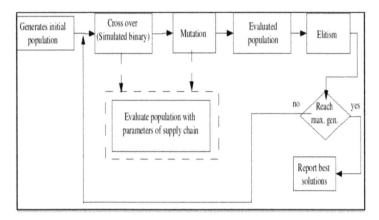

Figure 3 The cycle of genetic algorithm

a. Encoding a Chromosome

The chromosome should contain information about the solution it
represents. Several encoding are proposed:

- Binary encoding: One way of encoding is a binary string. The
chromosome could look like this:

Chromosome 1   1101100100110110

Chromosome 2   1101011000011110

Each bit in the string can represent some characteristic of the solution or it could
represents whether or not some particular characteristic was present.

✓   **Permutation Encoding:** Permutation encoding can be used in
ordering problems, such as the travelling salesman problem or a task ordering
problem. Every chromosome is a string of numbers, which represents number in
a sequence. In the TSP each number would represent a city to be visited.

Chromosome 1   1 4 7 9 6 3 5 0 2 8

Chromosome 2   9 3 2 5 8 1 6 0 4 7

✓ **Value Encoding:** Direct value encoding can be used in problems where some complicated values, such as real numbers, are used and where binary encoding would not suffice. While value encoding is very good for some problems, it is often necessary to develop some specific crossover and mutation techniques for these chromosomes.

Chromosome 1   A B E D B C A E D D

Chromosome 2   N W W N E S S W N N

In chromosome 1 above, A could represent a particular task, B another, etc.

✓ **Tree encoding:** Tree encoding is used to actually have programs or expressions evolve (see figure 4). In tree encoding every chromosome is a tree of some objects, such as functions or commands in the programming language.

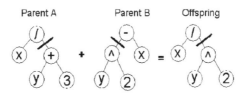

Figure 4 the Tree encoding

b. Selection

Selection is the stage of a genetic algorithm in which individual genomes are chosen from a population for later breeding (recombination or crossover). There are several genetic selection algorithms, such as tournament selection, rank selection and random selection.

✓ **Tournament selection:** is one of many methods of selection in genetic algorithms which runs a "tournament" among a few individuals chosen at random from the population and selects the winner (the one with the best fitness).If the tournament size is larger, weak individuals have a smaller chance to be selected [13].

✓ **Rank Selection:** Rank selection first ranks the population and then every chromosome receives fitness from this ranking. The worst will have fitness 1, second worst 2 etc. and the best will have fitness N (number of chromosomes in population).

✓ **Random Selection:** is a selection operator which randomly selects a chromosome from the population.

Since good individuals may be lost, the concept of Elitism copies the best chromosome (or a few best chromosomes) to the population in the next generation. The rest are chosen in classical way. Elitism can very rapidly increase performance of GA, because it prevents loosing the best found solution to date. A variation is to eliminate an equal number of the worst solutions, i.e. for each "best chromosome" carried over a "worst chromosome" is deleted.

c. Crossover

In genetic algorithms, **crossover** is a genetic operator used to vary the programming of a chromosome or chromosomes from one generation to the next. It is analogous to reproduction and biological crossover, upon which genetic algorithms are based. Many crossover techniques exist for organisms which use different data structures to store themselves [15].

✓ **Single Point Crossover :** Randomly choose a crossover point, then for offspring 1

a) copy everything in parent 1 before the crossover point and

b) copy everything in parent2 after this point to the new chromosome.

For offspring 2 do the reverse (see figure 5).

Parent A   Parent B   offspring

11001011+11011**111** = **11001111**

Figure 5 one point crossover

✓ **Two Point Crossover:** the operator is the same as above except this time two crossover points are randomly chosen (see figure 6).

Parent A   Parent B   offspring

11001011 + 11**011111** = **11011111**

Figure 6 Two point crossover

✓ **Uniform Crossover** A certain number of genes are randomly selected to be "swapped" (see figure).

Parent A   Parent B   offspring

11001011 + 11011101 = 11011111

Figure 7 Uniform crossover

✓ **Arithmetic Crossover:** Some arithmetic operation is performed on the two strings to create a new   string. In the example below (figure 8), a binary encoding and AND operator are used .

Parent A   Parent B   offspring

11001011 + 11011100 = 11001000 (AND)

Figure 8 Arithmetic crossover

d.   Mutation

In order to ensure that the individuals are not all exactly the same because the initial population may not contain enough variability to find the solution via crossover operations alone, the GA also uses a mutation operator where the chromosomes are randomly changed.

For the binary coding, the mutation is usually done on a bit-by-bit basis where a chosen bit is flipped from 0 to 1 (figure 9), or vice versa. Mutation of a given bit occurs with small probability p_m. Real-number coding requires a different type of mutation operator. That is, with a (0,1) based coding, an opposite is easily defined, but with a real number, there is no clearly defined opposite (e.g., it does not make sense to "flip" the 2.74 element)[10].

111101110

↓

111111110

Figure 9 Mutation for binary coding

So Mutation is an important part of the genetic search. It helps to prevent the population from stagnating at any local optima. Mutation occurs during evolution according to a user-definable mutation probability. This probability should usually be set fairly low (*0.01 is a good first choice*). If it is set to high, the search will turn into a primitive random search.

III.   *Evolutionary Algorithms for Multi-objective optimization*

In multi-objective optimization problems, there are several objectives to be minimized or maximized simultaneously. But, usually these objectives cannot minimize or maximize at the same time since there is a trade off relationship between the objectives. Since GAs are one of the multi-point search methods, they can discover simultaneously different solutions and thus they are suitable to solve multi-objective optimization problems.

Two major problems must be addressed when an evolutionary algorithm is applied to multi-objective optimization [17]:

▪ How to accomplish fitness assignment and selection, respectively, in order to guide the search towards the Pareto-optimal set.

▪ How to maintain a diverse population in order to prevent premature convergence.

III.1 Global Convergence

Roughly speaking, a Multi-objective Evolutionary algorithm is called globally convergent if the sequence of Pareto front approximations $A(t)$ it produces converges to the true Pareto front PF while the number of generations t goes to infinity. It is intuitively clear that this property can only be fulfilled with unlimited memory resources, as the cardinality of the Pareto front can be arbitrary large in general. Practical implementations, however, always have to deal with limited memory resources. In this case one is restricted to finding a subset of the Pareto front, and a globally convergent algorithm should guarantee

$$A(t) \rightarrow \acute{P}F \subseteq PF.$$

In the single-objective case, two conditions are sufficient to guarantee global convergence:

1. A strictly covering mutation distribution, which ensures that any solution $x^* \in X$ can be produced from every $x \in X$ by mutation with a positive probability,

2. An elitist (environmental) selection rule, which ensures that an optimal solution is not lost and no deterioration can occur.

While the mutation condition transfers easily to the multi-objective case, the elitist selection rule does not. This is due to the fact that a total order of the solutions is not given anymore and solutions can become incomparable to each other. If too many non-dominated solutions arise than can be stored in the population, some have to be discarded. This environmental selection strategy essentially determines whether an algorithm is globally convergent or not [22].

III.2   Diversity Preservation

Most MOEAs try to maintain diversity along the current approximation of the Pareto set by incorporating density information into the selection process: *an individuals chance of being selected is decreased the greater the density of individuals in its neighborhoods.* This issue is closely related to the estimation of probability density functions in statistics, and the methods used in MOEAs can be classified according to the categories of techniques used in statistical density estimation. Nearest neighbor techniques take the distance of a given point to its k_th nearest neighbor into account in order to estimate the density in its neighborhood. Usually, the estimator is a function of the inverse of this distance [22].

III.3 Archiving Strategies

Although diversity preservation techniques aim at guiding the population towards the Pareto-optimal set, still good solutions may be lost during the optimization process due to random effects. A common way to deal with this problem is to maintain a secondary population, the so-called archive, to which promising solutions in the population are copied at each generation (the concept of elitism). The archive may just be used as an external storage separate from the optimization engine or may be integrated into the EA by including archive members in the selection process [23].

Usually the size of the archive is restricted due to memory but also run-time limitations. Therefore, criteria on the basis of which the solutions to be kept in the archive are selected have to be defined. With this method, the best individuals in each generation are always preserved, and this helps the algorithm get close to its POF. *The dominance criterion is most commonly used, i.e., dominated archive members are removed and the archive comprises only the current approximation of the Pareto set.*

However, as this criterion is in general not sufficient (e.g., for continuous problems the Pareto set may contain an infinite number of solutions) additional information is taken into account *to reduce the number of archive members* further. Examples are *density information* and the time that has been passed since the individual entered the archive. Most elitist MOEAs make use of a *combination of dominance and density to choose the individuals that will be kept in the archive at every generation [4]*. Most algorithms under concern make use of a second population of elite individuals. The Strength Pareto EA (SPEA) [3], SPEA2[4] and NSGA2[7], are examples of this category.

We describe in the next paragraph some well known MOEA: NSGA[6], NSGA2[7], SPEA[3] and SPEA2[4].

IV. *Nondominated Sorting Genetic Algorithm (NSGA)*

The non-dominated sorting genetic algorithm was first implemented by Srinivas and Deb [6]. While it follows the standard genetic algorithm for parent selection and offspring generation, it determines the fitness of the individual using the concept of Pareto dominance as follows. First, the non-dominated individuals in the current population are identified. The same fitness value is assigned to all the non-dominated individuals. The individuals are then ignored temporarily, and the rest of the population is processed in the same way to identify a new set of non-dominated individuals.

A fitness value that is smaller than the previous one is assigned to all the individuals belonging to the second non-dominated front. This process continues until the whole population is classified into non-dominated fronts with different fitness values. In the original algorithm, the fitness is shared within the decision space.

V. *Non-dominated Sorting Genetic Algorithm II (NSGA II)*

NSGA-II successfully combines the following key element

1. A fast non-dominated sorting approach.

2. A density estimator.

3. A crowded comparison operator.

In the fast nondominated sorting approach, each solution is compared with every other solution in the population to find if it is dominated. First, all individuals in the first nondominated front are found. In order to find the individuals in the next front, the solutions in the first front are temporarily discounted. The procedure is repeated to find all the subsequent fronts.

To get an estimate of the density of solutions surrounding a particular point in the population the average distance of the two points on either side of this point along each of the objectives is adopted. The obtained quantity serves as an estimate of the size of the largest cuboid enclosing the point of interest, without including any other point in the population (the so-called crowding distance).The crowded comparison operator guides the selection process at the various stages of the algorithm towards an uniformly spread out Pareto-optimal front [7]. Between two solutions with different nondominated ranks, the point with the lower rank is always preferred. Otherwise, if both points belong to the same front, then the point which is located in a region with a lower number of points is preferred (the size of the cuboid enclosing it is larger).

In the algorithm's main loop,

- a random parent population P_0 is initially created.
- The population is sorted based on nondomination. Each solution is assigned a fitness equal to its nondomination level (1 is the best level). Thus, minimization of fitness is assumed.
- Binary tournament selection, recombination, and mutation operators are used to create a child population Q_0 of size N.
- From the first generation onward, the procedure is different. First, a combined population $R_t = P_t \cup Q_t$ is formed. The population R_t will be of size $2N$. Then, the population R_t is sorted according to nondomination.
- The new parent population P_{t+1} is formed by adding at first solutions from the first front .Thereafter , the solutions of the following fronts . The solution of the last accepted front are sorted according to the crowded comparison operator and the first points are picked until the size of P_{t+1} reaches N.

This is how the population P_{t+1} of size N is constructed. This population of size N is now used for selection, crossover and mutation to create a new population Q_{t+1} of size N.

Algorithm 1: NSGA-II (main loop)

while *not stopping rule* **do**

Let $R_t = P_t \cup Q_t$;

Let F = fast-non-dominated-sort (R_t);

Let $P_{t+1} = \emptyset$ *and* $i = 1$;

while $/ P_{t+1} / + /F_i/ < N$ **do**

Apply crowding-distance-assignment (F_i);

Let $P_{t+1} = P_{t+1} \cup F_i$;

Let $i = i + 1$;

end

Sort(Fi, $< n$);

Let $P_{t+1} = P_{t+1} \cup F_i [1 : (N - / P_{t+1} /)]$;

Let Q_{t+1} = make-new- pop(P_{t+1});

Let $t = t + 1$;

End

VI.   *Strength Pareto Evolutionary Algorithm (SPEA)*

SPEA, an acronym for Strength Pareto Evolutionary Algorithm, was among the first techniques that are extensively compared to several existing evolution-based methods [3]. As it clearly outperformed the (non elitist) alternative approaches under consideration, it has been used as a point of reference by various researchers. SPEA uses a regular population and an archive (external set). Starting with an initial population and an empty archive the following steps are performed per iteration.

First, all non-dominated population members are copied to the archive; any dominated individuals or duplicates (regarding the objective values) are removed from the archive during this update operation. If the size of the updated archive exceeds a predefined limit, further archive members are deleted by a clustering technique which preserves the characteristics of the non-dominated front. Afterwards, fitness values are assigned to both archive and population members:

- Each individual i in the archive is assigned a strength value $S(i) \in [0; 1)$, which at the same time represents its fitness value $F(i)$. $S(i)$ is the number of population members j that are dominated by or equal to i with respect to the objective values, divided by the population size plus one.

-The fitness $F(j)$ of an individual j in the population is calculated by summing the strength values $S(i)$ of all archive members i that dominate or are equal to j, and adding one at the end [3].

The next step represents the mating selection phase where individuals from the union of population and archive are selected by means of binary tournaments (fitness is to be minimized here, i.e., each individual in the archive has a higher chance to be selected than any population member). Finally, after recombination and mutation the old population is replaced by the resulting offspring population .

VII.   *Strength Pareto Evolutionary Algorithm II(SPEA II)*

The Strength Pareto Evolutionary Algorithm (SPEA) of Zitzler & Thiele (1999) is a well-established Pareto-optimization algorithm, which uses the dominance criterion for the fitness assignment and selection of solutions SPEA2 is presented to eliminate the potential weaknesses of its predecessor and to incorporate most recent results in order to design a powerful and up-to-date MOEA algorithm. SPEA2 uses two populations. External population is initially empty. After fitness evaluation, all non-dominated solutions from current population and from external population are passed in the next population. If the number of these solutions is less than population size than the next population is filled with dominated individuals from current and external population [4].

The fitness function is differently calculated for the solutions from the external and current populations. In contrast to SPEA, SPEA2 uses a fine grained fitness assignment strategy. This *incorporates density information* to discriminate between individuals having identical fitness values. *The archive size is fixed.* Whenever the number of non-dominated individuals is less than the predefined archive size, the archive is filled up by dominated individuals.

The clustering technique (which SPEA uses when the non-dominated front exceeds the archive limit) has been replaced by an alternative truncation method. This truncation method does not loose boundary points. Another difference with respect to SPEA is that only members of the archive participate in the mating selection process. The SPEA2 algorithm is given here below:

Input:

N (population size)

$\bar{N}$ *(archive size)*

T (maximum number of generations)

Output: *A (nondominated set)*

Step 1: *Initialization*: *Generate an initial population p_0 and create the empty archive (external set)* $\overline{p_0} = \phi$. *Set $t = 0$.*

Step 2: *Fitness assignment*: *Calculate fitness values of individuals in p_t and $\overline{p_t}$*

Step 3: *Environmental selection*: *Copy all nondominated individuals in p_t and $\overline{p_t}$ to $\overline{p_{t+1}}$.*

If size of $\overline{p_{t+1}}$ exceeds $\bar{N}$ then reduce $\overline{p_{t+1}}$ by means of the truncation operator, otherwise if size of $\overline{p_{t+1}}$ is less than N then fill $\overline{p_{t+1}}$ with dominated individuals in p_t and $\bar{p}_t$.

Step 4: *Termination*: *If $t \geq T$ or another stopping criterion is satisfied then set A to the set of decision vectors represented by the nondominated individuals in $\overline{p_{t+1}}$. Stop.*

Step 5: *Mating selection: Perform binary tournament selection with replacement on $\overline{p_{t+1}}$ in order to fill the mating pool.*

Step 6: *Variation: Apply recombination and mutation operators to the mating pool and set p_{t+1} to the resulting population. Increment generation counter ($t = t + 1$) and go to Step 2.*

- **Fitness Assignment**

To avoid the situation that individuals dominated by the same archive members have identical fitness values, with SPEA2 for each individual both dominating and dominated solutions are taken into account.

In detail, each individual i in the archive $\overline{p_t}$ *and* the population p_t is assigned a strength value $S(i)$, representing the number of solutions it dominates :

$$S(i)=|\{j \mid j \in p_t \cup \overline{p_t} \ ^\wedge i \vdash j\}|; \quad (10)$$

On the basis of the S values, the raw fitness $R(i)$ of an individual i is calculated:

$$R(i)=\sum_{j \in p_t \cup \overline{p_t} \ ^\wedge j \vdash i} S(j); \quad (11)$$

Therefore, additional density information is incorporated to discriminate between individuals having identical raw fitness values. The density estimation technique used in SPEA2 is an adaptation of the k-th nearest neighbor method [24], where the density at any point is a (decreasing) function of the distance to the k-th nearest data point.

Here, we simply take the inverse of the distance to the k-th nearest neighbor as the density estimate. To be more precise, for each individual i the distances (in objective space) to all individuals j in archive and population are calculated and stored in a list. After sorting the list in increasing order, the k-th element gives the distance sought, denoted as θ_i^k. We use $k = \left|\sqrt{N + \overline{N}}\right|$. Afterwards, the density $D(i)$ corresponding to i is defined by

$$D(i) = \frac{1}{1 + \theta_i^k}; \quad (12)$$

Finally, adding $D(i)$ to the raw fitness value $R(i)$ of an individual I yields its fitness $F(i)$: $\qquad F(i) = R(i) + D(i); \qquad (13)$

32

- **Environmental Selection**

During environmental selection, the first step is to copy all non-dominated individuals, i.e., those which have a fitness lower than one, from archive and population to the archive of the next generation:

$$\overline{p_{t+1}} = \{i \mid i \in p_t \cup \overline{p_t} \wedge f(i) < 1\}; \qquad (14)$$

If the non-dominated front fits exactly into the archive ($|\overline{p_{t+1}}| = \overline{N}$) the environmental selection step is completed. Otherwise, there can be two situations: Either the archive is too small ($|\overline{p_{t+1}}| < \overline{N}$) or too large ($|\overline{p_{t+1}}| > \overline{N}$).

- In the first case, the best $\overline{N} - |\overline{p_{t+1}}|$ dominated individuals in the previous archive and population are copied to the new archive.

- In the second case, when the size of the current non-dominated (multi) set exceeds $\overline{N}$, an archive truncation procedure is invoked which iteratively removes individuals from $\overline{p_{t+1}}$ until $\lceil \overline{p_{t+1}} \rceil = \overline{N}$.

Here, at each iteration that individual I is chosen for removal for which

$$i \leq_d j \, for \qquad all \quad j \in \overline{p_{t+1}}$$

$$with$$

$$i \leq_d j: \qquad \forall \, 0 < k < \lceil \overline{p_{t+1}} \rceil : \theta_i^k = \theta_j^k$$

$$or$$

$$\exists \, 0 < k < \lceil \overline{p_{t+1}} \rceil : \, [(\, \forall \, 0 < l < k : \, \theta_i^l = \theta_j^l) \wedge \theta_i^k < \theta_j^k] \, ; \, (15)$$

where θ_i^k denotes the distance of i to its k-th nearest neighbor in $\overline{p_{t+1}}$.

VIII.   Conclusion

NSGA2 and SPEA2 are quite similar in the way they operate and in terms of using elitism. However, they are made different by the ways in which they preserve elitism [22]. The details are summarized in table 1

	NSGA2	SPEA2
External set	- might include dominated solutions based on dominance-ranking - Fixed size: initial population size - Truncation: based on crowding distance	- might include dominated solutions based on fitness value related to density information - Fixed size: population size preferable - Truncation: based on k-th nearest distance
Selection for reproduction	Crowded binary tournament selection based on the rank and crowding distance	Binary tournament selection on fitness value related to density information

Table 1 Differences between NSGA2 and SPEA2.

MOEA are very powerful algorithms but they need a large computation time when dealing with large combinational optimization problems .This several approaches are proposed to distribute them.

Chapter 3

Study of the performance of
the Balanced Explore Exploit Distributed
Evolutionary Algorithm
"BEEDEA"
on the multiobjective knapsack problem

I.   Introduction

Evolutionary Algorithms (EAs) are efficient heuristic search methods with powerful characteristics of robustness and flexibility to capture global solutions of complex optimization problems. Using EAs the probability of finding a near optimum in an early stage of the optimization process is very high. For that reason, parallelizing EAs is an important issue. Since we are looking for a number of Pareto-optimal solutions with different tradeoffs between the objectives, it seems natural to assign different parts of the search space to different processors. The parallel architectures permit to get some very satisfactory results in parallelizing EAs.

II.   Parallel Multi-objective Evolutionary Algorithms

Parallel genetic algorithms are roughly classified into three categories: master-slave population model, island model, and cellular model.

II.1 Master-Slave

As in most evolutionary algorithms the fitness evaluation of the individuals is the most computation intensive part, it is self-evident to distribute this operation to different processors. The master works on the same population as the serial EA would, but delegates the fitness evaluation of an individual to another processor. After this evaluation, the fitness value is returned back to a shared memory, or is communicated through message passing, which allows the master to read the values. The environmental selection and the mating selection is done by the master process. Master-slaves models can be implemented in two different ways: synchronous and asynchronous:

✓ In the synchronous model the master delegates the fitness evaluations to the slave processors and waits until the fitness of every individual of the population has been computed. Thereafter, it performs the selection and the variation.

✓ By contrast, the master of an asynchronous master-slave model delegates the fitness computations and doesn't wait for the whole population to be evaluated. The newly evaluated individuals are directly added to the population and it undergoes selection and variation even if not the entire population is evaluated.

The results of a synchronous master-slave parallelization don't differ from the results of a serial EA, because the performed algorithm is the same. Unlike the synchronous model, the asynchronous model produces different results, due to the algorithmic changes[8].

II.2 Island Model

One can observe in nature that the overall diversity is maintained through isolation, meaning that mating and environmental selection happen separately for each subpopulation. In nature this isolation is due to geographical constraints like valleys and islands, which delimit the mobility of the individuals. As this concept of several small subpopulations (also called demes), helped the biota to develop, it has been ported to evolutionary algorithms, where it is called island models (IM).

Island models split up the population and the isolation of the demes is achieved by running a separate EA on each subpopulation.

Parallelization comes in, because these different islands can easily be run on several computers at the same time. As complete isolation of the islands would be disadvantageous, from time to time individuals have to be exchanged between the subpopulations. This step is called migration. A well balanced migration lets the information of good individuals pass among the islands but helps also to preserve diversity by isolation of the different islands.

In comparison to normal EAs, this differentiation of the subpopulations can be advantageous over the case with just one big population (panmictic EA), because the problems search space is explored more evenly and the overall diversity helps to fight population stagnation [8].

II.3 Cellular model

In this model, the population is divided into many and small demes, often thousands. In the simplest case one can use a single large population with one string per processor. Usually each processor controls one or a small amount of individuals and there is intensive communication between demes. The individuals belonging to the whole population are distributed topologically in a grid and are restricted to reproduce in a small environment of its location. Selection and mating are local with neighbors. A critical parameter is the ratio between the radius of the deme and the size of the underlying grid [2].

III. Balanced Explore-Exploit clustering based Distributed Evolutionary Algorithm for multi-objective optimization (BEEDEA)

BEEDEA is a parallel multi-objective evolutionary algorithm based on an island model [1]. According to this algorithm, the distribution of individuals among the available processors is motivated by the fact that the efficiency of the search process is related to obtaining a good balance between the two main search mechanisms: **exploitation and exploration [1]**.

The exploitation permits to explore regions of the search space near of those visited earlier that have good quality. However, **the exploration** tries to direct the search process toward the unvisited regions or the less explored regions. It permits to generate solutions that defer meaningfully of those previously visited. Extreme exploitation can lead to premature convergence and intense exploration can make the search ineffective. The basic idea of this parallel scheme is to re-distribute individuals of the global population enabling efficient global and local searches to be performed.

The BEEDEA is based on an island model. It gathers the global population at regular intervals. Then, it divides the search space by clustering algorithms. A clustering technique is used here to obtain a partitioning of the search space that depends on the distribution of individuals in the search/objective space. Finally, the found clusters are redistributed among processors such that both global exploration and local exploration (exploitation) will be performed. In fact, the BEEDEA executes in turn an exploration step and an exploitation step (figure 15).

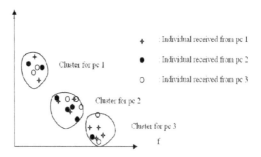

Figure 10 Clustering for the exploitation step with 3 processors

In the *exploitation* step, the global population is partitioned into p clusters (p is the number of processor used for the distribution). Then, each processor receives one cluster. Each sub-population evolves on its processor for a few generations.

In the *exploration* step, the population is divided into 2p clusters. Each processor receives two distinct clusters. Then, a crossover stage between pairs of individuals each one of them belonging to one cluster is performed. After that an elitist MOEA will be performed for few generations.

The main algorithm consists of two kinds of processes, an organizer and several elitist MOEA. There is only one organizer, with the responsibility of collecting the different sub-populations from the other processors, clustering the global population and redistributing the obtained clusters between all processors (the organizer and the others).

The model can be explained as follow:

Interval <-- 0

Step 1: Initialize sub-population is performed randomly. The global population size is N. The size of each sub-population is N/P (p is the processor number).

Step 2: An elitist MOEA is performed for some generations.

Step 3: All the individuals are gathered by the organizer. Then the global Pareto front found is given.

Step 4: A clustering algorithm is performed on the global population. The number of cluster is equal to p if exploitation step, to 2p otherwise.

Interval <-- Interval +1

If Interval mod 2=0 then go to **step 5** else go to **step 6**.

Step 5: Exploitation step: Each processor receives one cluster. Each processor will execute an elitist MOEA for some iterations. Go to step 3.

Step 6: Exploration step: each process receives two distinct clusters and a crossover step between pairs of individuals each one from one cluster is performed and then an elitist MOEA runs for some generations. Go to step 3[1].

A clustering algorithm is used to partition the population of obtained individuals into a given number of homogenous groups. Building similarity groups in the objective space is interesting, because members of a group will have close scores in the different objectives (that are directly linked with the optimization problem). BEEDEA uses an *agglomerative hierarchical clustering algorithm.* For example, suppose this data is to be clustered, and the Euclidean distance is the distance metric.

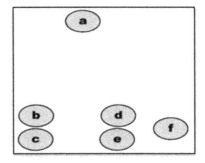

Figure 11 Agglomerative hierarchical clustering: Raw Data

The hierarchical clustering dendrogram would be as such:

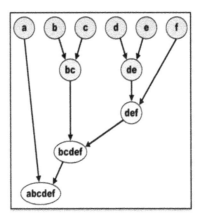

Figure 12 Agglomerative hierarchical clustering: Traditional representation

This method builds the hierarchy from the individual elements by progressively merging clusters. In our example, we have six elements {a} {b} {c} {d} {e} and {f}. The first step is to determine which elements to merge in a cluster. BEEDEA takes the two closest elements, according to the chosen distance

(Euclidean distance). BEEDEA stops the hierarchy when the desired number of clusters is obtained. BEEDEA uses an elitist MOEA which run on each processor which is the SPEA.

IV. *Some improvement on BEEDEA*

BEEDEA uses a SPEA on each processor, but SPEA presents some weaknesses that can be repaired by SPEA2, in fact, SPEA2 is able to eliminate the potential weaknesses of its predecessor SPEA. The main differences of SPEA2 in comparison to SPEA are:

- An improved fitness assignment scheme is used in SPEA2, which takes for each individual into account how many individuals it dominates and it is dominated by. In SPEA, individuals that are dominated by the same archive members have identical fitness values. That means in the case when the archive contains only a single individual, all population members have the same rank independently of whether they dominate each other or not [4]. As a consequence, the selection pressure is decreased substantially and in this particular case SPEA behaves like a random search algorithm.

- A nearest neighbor density estimation technique is incorporated which allows a more precise guidance of the search process. If many individuals of the current generation are indifferent, i.e., do not dominate each other, density information has to be used in order to guide the search more effectively [4]. Clustering makes use of this information, but only with regard to the archive and not to the population.

- A new archive truncation method which guarantees the preservation of boundary solutions is introduced into SPEA2. Although the clustering technique used in SPEA is able to reduce the non-dominated set without destroying its characteristics, it may lose outer solutions. However, these solutions should be kept in the archive in order to obtain a good spread of non-dominated solutions.

- In contrast to SPEA, SPEA2 uses a fine-grained fitness assignment strategy which incorporates density information.

Furthermore, the archive size is fixed, i.e., whenever the number of nondominated individuals is less than the predefined archive size, the archive is filled up by dominated individuals; with SPEA, the archive size may vary over time.

- Another difference with respect to SPEA is that only members of the archive participate in the mating selection process.

SPEA2 was implemented in [4] , and it shows to constitute a significant improvement over its predecessor SPEA as it reaches better results on all considered problems, for this reason, SPEA is replaced by SPEA2 in our algorithm BEEDEA.

In BEEDEA, the global population (all dominated and non-dominated solutions) is gathered in the master processor. Since only solutions in the archive are selected in the mating pool in SPEA2, then at each interval only the archive of each island is sent to the master process. Thus the clustering is performed only on the global archive.

V. The multi-objective knapsack problem

The knapsack problem is a combinatorial optimization problem. It derives its name from the maximization problem of the best choice of essentials that can fit into one bag to be carried on a trip. The decision problem form of the knapsack problem is the question "can a value of at least V be achieved without exceeding the weight W?". Similar problem often appears in business, complexity theory, cryptography and applied mathematics.

V.1 The 0/1 knapsack problem

Generally, a **0/1 knapsack problem** consists of a set of items, weight and profit associated with each item, and an upper bound for the capacity of the knapsack. The task is to find a subset of items which maximizes the total of the profits in the subset, yet all selected items fit into the knapsack, i.e., the total weight does not exceed the given capacity. Suppose we have n kinds of items, 1 through n. Each kind of item j has a value p_j and a weight w_j. The maximum weight that we can carry in the bag is W.

The **0-1 knapsack problem** restricts the number x_j of copies of each kind of item to zero or $\leq$one. Mathematically the 0-1-knapsack problem can be formulated as:

$$\text{Maximize } \sum_{j=1}^{n} p_j x_j$$

$$\text{Subject to } \sum_{j=1}^{n} w_j x_j \leq w, \quad x_j \in \{0, 1\}$$

V.2 The multi-objective knapsack problem

The single-objective **knapsack** problem can be extended directly to the multi-objective case by associating m different profit and m different weight values per item and m capacity bounds. The multi-objective knapsack problem is one of the most extensively used benchmark problem for multi-objective metaheuristics.

Given a set of n items, each of which has m profit and m weight values associated with it. The goal is to select a subset of items such that the sums over each of their m-th weight values do not exceed given bounds and the sums over each of their m-th profit values are maximized. The m-th objective function value of a solution (set of items) is then defined as the sum over their m-th profit values. A solution is feasible, if each of the m summation over their m-th weight values does not exceed the m-th capacity bound.

Formally, the multi-objective 0/1 knapsack problem is defined [5] in the following way: Given a set of m items and a set of n knapsacks, with

$p_{i,j}$ =profit of items j according to knapsack i

$w_{i,j}$=weight of items j according to knapsack i

c_i=capacity of knapsack i

Find a vector $x=(x_1, x_2, \ldots, x_m) \in \{0,1\}^m$, such that

$$\forall i \in \{1,2 \ldots, n\} : \sum_{j=1}^{m} w_{i,j} x_j \leq c_i$$

and for which $f(x)=(f(x)_1, f_2(x), ..., f_n(x))$ is maximum , Where

$$f_i(x)=\sum_{j=1}^{m} p_{i,j} x_j$$

and $x_j = 1$ if item j is selected.

A test problem for a comparative investigation like this has to be chosen carefully. The problem should be understandable and easy to formulate so that the experiments are repeatable and verifiable. It should also be a rather general problem and ideally represent a certain class of real-world problems.

Both conditions apply to the knapsack problem: the problem description is simple, yet the problem itself is difficult to solve (NP-hard). Moreover, the multi-objective knapsack problem is one of the most extensively used benchmark problem for multi-objective metaheuristics, this is why it is chosen to be our test problem for a comparative investigation.

V.3 Design of the genetic resolution

A representation as a pseudo-Boolean optimization problem is typically used, where the n binary decision variables denote whether an item is selected or not. However, solutions fail on problems with restrictive capacities. A greedy repair method is used. This method is based on a vector representation and repairs infeasible solutions according to a predefined scheme. A simple repair method is applied to the genotype: the repair algorithm removes items from the solution coded step by step until all capacity constraints are fulfilled. The order in which the items are deleted is determined by the maximum profit/weight ratio per item; for item the maximum profit/weight ratio is given by this equation:

$$q_{j=} \max_{i=1} \left\{ \frac{p_{i,j}}{wi,j} \right\}$$

We have used tournament selection, one point crossover and uniform mutation.

VI. Implementation and Results

In this chapter we study the evolutionary algorithm BEEDEA on the mlti-objective Knapsack problem. BEEDEA is compared to a sequential SPEA2 and PSPEA2 which is a parallel island model without migration.

VI.1. The material and software tools

- **Software tools:** The software of the work environment are:

- The operating system: professional Windows xp version 2002.

- The software of programming: visual studio version 6.0.

- The software GUIMMO: Graphical User Interface Multi-Objective Optimization (see annexes A).

- MPICH: The environment of MPI programming developed by Mathematics and Computer Science Division in Argonne National Laboratory it serves to establish the communication between the different processors (see annexes B).

-Microsoft Office word 2007: software for treatment texts.

- **Material tools**
- ✓ Performances of PC and the environment work space :
- Processor Intel Pentium 4 CPU 3.00 GHZ 3.01 GHZ.
- 512 Mb of random-access memory.
- Hard disk's capacity 80 GB.

VI.2 Implemented algorithms

All these algorithms are implemented using the c ++ language and the communication between the different processors is supported by MPI.

- ✓ SPEA 2
- ✓ PSPEA2
- ✓ BEEDED

VI.3 Performance Metrics

Three complementary performance indicators have been used for evaluating
the quality of the obtained non-dominated sets: the *entropy* and the *contribution.*
The *entropy* indicator gives an idea about the diversity of the solutions found.
Whereas the *contribution* indicator compares two fronts in terms of dominance
(The contribution metric quantifies the dominance between two Pareto optimal
sets) (see annexes A). We have used also the generational distance. The
optimization is performed for 5 simulations and we considered the average of
these values.

VI.4 Test problems

We have tested our algorithm on the benchmark sets of Zitzler[25]. Four
problems are considered while varying the number of items and the number of
knapsacks(Table 2)

	Number of items	Number of knapsacks
A	100	4
B	750	4
C	500	4
D	250	4

Table 2 test problems

VI.5 The different results

In this test, we compare the results of the execution of SPEA2, PSPEA2 and BEEDEA, in order to study the benefits of parallelism for the MOEAs and to compare the results given by PSPEA2 and those given by BEEDEA.

❖ *Evaluation of the 2 models: SPEA2, PSPEA2*

Parameters used:

✓ probability of mutation: 0.01
✓ size of the global population :   100
✓ size of the population archives: 100
✓ number of generation :   48
        For PSPEA2:
✓   number of processor : 8

▪ First case
✓   number of items: 750
✓ Number of knapsack: 4

Contribution	SPEA2	PSPEA2
SPEA2	0	0.218
PSPEA2	0.781	0

Table 3 Contribution SPEA2 versus PSPEA2 for the 750.4 knapsack problem

It is clear that PSPEA2 outperforms the SPEA2 according to contribution measure. PSPEA2 converges better to the true Pareto front.

▪ Second case
✓   number of items: 500
✓   Number of knapsack: 4

Contribution	SPEA2	PSPEA2
SPEA2	0	0.142
PSPEA2	0.857	0

Table 4 Contribution SPEA2 versus PSPEA2 for the 500.4 knapsack problem.

The parallel algorithm PSPEA2 explores better the search space. The use of several sub-populations improves the diversity of the global population. The nondominated set fend by PSPEA2 dominates almost all the one fend by SPEA2 .

- Third case:
✓ number of items: 250
✓ Number of knapsack: 4

Contribution	SPEA2	PSPEA2
SPEA2	0	0.333
PSPEA	0.666	0

Table 5 Contribution SPEA2 versus PSPEA2 for the 250.4 knapsack problem

We can conclude, from these tables, that a considerable number of solutions given by SPEA2 are dominated by PSPEA2(only 0.218 per cent of SPEA2's solutions are not dominated by PSPEA2 in the 250.4 knapsack problem), this results assure the utility to use the concept of parallelism that generates more non-dominated solutions.

❖ *Evaluation of the 3 models: SPEA2, PSPEA2 and BEEDEA*

Parameters used:

✓ probability of mutation: 0.01
✓ size of the global population : 100
✓ size of the population archives: 100

For BEEDEA

✓ number of processor : 2
✓ number of intervals : 3
✓ number of generation of intensification: 2
✓ number of generation of diversification: 2

For PSPEA2:

✓ number of processor : 2
✓ number of intervals: 7

Contribution

Contribution	SEA2	PSPEA2	BEEDEA
SPEA2	0	0.3461	0.5162
PSPEA2	0.6538	0	0.6296
BEEDEA	0.4838	0.3703	0

Table 6 Contribution results for the knapsack 750.4

Entropy

Entropy	SPEA2	PSPEA2	BEEDEA
SPEA2	0	0.4321	0.4471
PSPEA2	0.4625	0	0.4512
BEEDEA	0.3780	0.3701	0

Table 7 Entropy results for the knapsack 750.4

According to the contribution measure PSPEA2 outperforms both SPEA2 and BEEDEA since C(PSPEA2,SPEA2)=0.6538 and C(PSPEA2,BEEDEA) =0.6296. BEEDEA performs SPEA2 near result to SPEA2 but it is dominated by PSPEA2 according to the contribution metric.

According to the entropy, PSPEA2 generates more diversified solutions than the BEEDEA and SPEA2. A butter adjustment of the parameters and the size of exploration and exploitation intervals is required to improve the results of BEEDEA.

❖ *The influence of mutation: We examined in this part the effect of the mutation's values*.

- The problem : knapsack.750.4 (750 items ,4 knapsacks)
    - ✓ number of processor : 2
    - ✓ number of intervals : 9
    - ✓ size of the global population : 100
    - ✓ size of the population archives: 100
    - ✓ number of generation of intensification: 2
    - ✓ number of generation of diversification: 2

Contribution:

Mutation's values	0.15	0.09
0.09	0.6911	0
0.15	0	0.3089

Table 8 Contribution results for the 750.4 knapsack problem and pm=0.15, 0.09

Entropy:

Mutation's values	0.15	0.09
0.09	0.3772	0
0.15	0	0.4089

Table 9 Entropy results for the 750.4 knapsack problem and pm=0.15, 0.09

From the values of contribution, we can conclude that most of the solutions given by a probability of mutation equal to 0.15 are dominated by the solutions given by the second value of mutation. A big value of mutation probability permits to direct research toward more exploration of the space what returns research similar to a random search. In the contrary case the algorithm directs toward the exploitation of the space and we risk in this condition that the algorithm doesn't converge. Mutation's probability is an important parameter in evolutionary algorithms and it is necessary to choose it carefully.

❖ *Study of the complementarily between Intensification and diversification*
   The different configuration
      ✓The problem : knapsack.250.2 (250 items ,2 knapsacks)

✓ number of processor : 2

✓ number of intervals : 3

✓ mutation : 0.01

✓ size of the global population : 100

✓ size of the population archives: 100

We study the three following configurations:

	number of generation of intensification	number of generation of diversification
A	8	0
B	0	8
C	8	8

Table 10 The configuration of BEEDEA

Contribution:

contribution	A	B	C
A	0	0,6271	0
B	0.3729	0	0
C	1	1	0

Table 11 study of BEEDEA: contribution

Entropy:

entropy	A	B	C
A	0	0.473	0.4878
B	0.3159	0	0.408
C	0.6068	0.06068	0

Table 12 study of BEEDEA: Entropy

When we examine the two tables, we notice that the Pareto fronts given by the configuration A and the one of the configuration B are completely dominated by the those given by the configuration C. From these results it is well clear that the balance between the intensification and the diversification gives best solutions. The same result is confirmed by the entropy measure where the Pareto set found by the configuration C is more diversified.

Conclusion

The study of the algorithm BEEDEA puts in evidence the interest of the integrating the phase of exploitation and the phase of exploration within a same algorithm.

BEEDEA slightly improve the SPEA2 on the knapsack considered problems. Other experiments are essential to the fine tuning off the BEEDEA parameters in order to reprove the results.

General Conclusion

This project was a good occasion to improve my knowledge in the domain of parallel computing, multi-objective optimization and evolutionary computation. This project was an opportunity to discover the research filed of distributed nature computing. The main objective was to study and improve the BEEDEA which is a distributed multi-objective evolutionary algorithm based on the balance between the exploration and the exploitation of the research space. During this work, I have studied the concept of parallelization of the evolutionary algorithms that is a good technique to solve the problems of optimization.

I have tested this algorithm after improving it by replacing the use of SPEA by the SPEA2 as basic elitist multi-objective evolutionary algorithm. I succeed to apply this algorithm to a complex problem that is the multi-objective knapsack.

The domain of meta-heuristic and parallel computing is a domain so vast and the applications made in this domain showed their capacities to the resolutions of the real – world problems. I hope finally to complete in this direction specially because I like both mathematics and computer science. So, I like to integrate the nature computing techniques and the distributed computing to solve such so complex problems by my own applications.

Annexes

Annex A

METRIC OF GUIMOO

- **The contribution [Meunier, 2002]**

The contribution (Ratio of Non Dominated Individuals) measure is obtained by comparing two sets of non-dominated individuals PO1 and PO2. At first, PO2 and PO1 are mixed then the contribution of the set PO1 is determined as the ratio of the number of non-dominated solutions in PO1 which are still non-dominated in the union of PO1 and PO2 by the total number of the solutions.

Example:

For example, we evaluate the contribution of the two sets of solutions PO1 of PO2 of Fig. 1: solutions of PO1 (resp. PO2) are represented by circles (resp. crosses). We have C(PO1, PO2) = 0.7 and C(PO2, PO1) = 0.3.

Figure 1 Example of contribution

- **Entropy [Basseur et al., 2002]**

The entropy metric quantifies the goodness of a set of solutions in terms of distribution quality over the Pareto frontier. The higher the entropy is, the more diversified the nondominated solutions are.

Let PO1 and PO2 be two sets of solutions.

• Let PO* be the set of optimal Pareto solutions of PO1 ∪ PO2.

• Let Ni be the cardinality of solutions of PO1 ∪ PO* which are in the niche of the ith solution of PO1 ∪ PO*.

• Let n_i be the cardinality of solutions of PO1 which are in the niche of the ith solution of PO1 ∪ PO*.

• Let C be the cardinality of the solutions of PO1 ∪ PO*.

• Let $Y = \sum_{i=1}^{c} \frac{1}{N_i}$ be the sum of the coefficients affected to each solution.

The more concentrated is a region of the solution space, the lower will be the coefficients of its solutions.Then, the following formula is applied to evaluate the entropy E of PO1, relatively to the space occupied by PO*:

$$E(PO_1, PO_2) = \frac{-1}{\log(Y)} \sum_{i=1}^{c} \left(\frac{1}{N_i} \frac{n_i}{c} \log \frac{n_i}{c} \right) \qquad (1)$$

• **Generational distance [Van Veldhuizen, 1999]**

This metric calculates the average of the solution, it permits to measure how far of the surface of compromises is located a set of solutions.

$$DG(A) = \frac{\left(\sum_{i=1}^{|P_A|} d_i^p \right)^{\frac{1}{p}}}{|P_A|} \qquad (2)$$

For p=2, d_i is the Euclidean distance (in the objectives space) between the solution i ∈ PA and the nearest element of P*:

$$d_i = \min_{k=1} \sqrt{\sum_{j=1}^{n}(f_j^i - f_j^k)^2} \quad \forall 1 \le k \le |P*| \quad (3)$$

- **The spacing metric**

The spacing metric gives a good indication of how evenly the solutions are distributed in the objective space. It is defined as:

$$S = \sqrt{\frac{1}{|P_A|} \sum_{i=1}^{|P_A|}(d_i - \bar{d})^2} \quad (4)$$

Where $\quad d_i = \min_{k \ne i \wedge k \in P_A} \sum_{m=1}^{n}|f_m^i - f_m^k| \quad (5)$

And $\quad \bar{d} = \frac{(\sum_{j=1}^{n} d_j)}{n} \quad (15)$

and n is the number of solutions in the current front PA. d_i is the Euclidian distance in the objective space between the solution i in PA and its nearest solution in the Pareto Optimal Front (POF). The smaller the spacing is, the more regularly distributed the solutions in PO are.

- **Coverage [Zitzler, 1999]**

Using metric C two sets of nondominated solutions can be compared to each other. Let X be the set of decision vectors for the considered problem and A,B $\subseteq$ X two sets of decision vectors. The function C maps the ordered pair (A, B) into the interval [0,1].

$$C(A, B) = \frac{|\{b \in B | \exists a \in A : a \vdash b\}|}{|B|} \quad (6)$$

Example

There are situations when the metric C cannot decide if an obtained front is better than the other. Let us suppose that front1 correspond to a set A and front 2 to a set B.

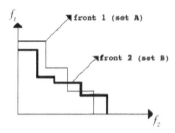

Figure 2 Example of coverage between 2 fronts

In Fig. 2, the surface covered by the front 1 is equal to the surface covered by the front 2 but front 2 is closer to the Pareto optimal front than front 1. In this situation (and in other situations similar with this) the C metric is not applicable. To eliminate this shortcoming a new metric D metric was proposed.

- **Coverage difference**

Let A, B $\subseteq$ X be two sets of decision vectors. The size of the space dominated by A and not dominated by B (regarding the objective space) is denoted D (A, B) and is defined as:

$$D (A, B) = S(A + B) - S(B) \qquad (7)$$

where S(A) is defined above.

Example

Metric D can be used to solve the inconvenience of Example. Consider the notations from Figure. By applying metric D the followings equalities are obtained:

$$S(A + B) = \alpha + \beta + \gamma$$

$$S(A) = \alpha + \gamma$$

$S(B) = \alpha + \beta$

The metric D for this example is expressed below.

$D(A,B) = \gamma$

$D(B,A) = \beta$

From $D(A,B) < D(B,A)$ it results that front 2 dominates front 1.

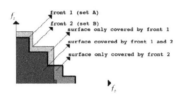

Figure 3: Example of difference between C metric and D metric for
considered fronts front 1 and front 2.

Zitzler (1999) suggests that (ideally) the D metric is used in
combination with the S metric where the values may be normalized by a reference
volume V , where (for a maximization problem) V is given by:

$$V = \prod_{i=1}^{k}(f_i^{max} - f_i^{min})$$

f_i^{max} and f_i^{min}i represent the maximum respectively minimum value for the
objective f_i. Thus, the value

$$D(\acute{A}, B) = \frac{D(A,B)}{V} \qquad (8)$$

represents the relative size of the region (in the objective space) dominated by A
and not dominated by B.

- **Size of the dominated space [Zitzler, 1999]**

The S metric measures how much of the objective space is dominated
by a given nondominated set A.

Presentation

Let X be set of decision vectors for the considered problem and

A = x1, x2, ..., xt ⊑ X a set of t decision vectors. The function S(A) gives the volume enclosed by the union of the polytopes p1, p2, ..., pt, where each pi is formed by the intersection of the following hyperplanes arising out of xi, along with the axes:

for each axis in the objective space there exist a hyperplane perpendicular to the axis and passing through the point (f1(xi), f2(xi), ..., fk(xi)).

Example

In the two-dimensional case, each pi represents a rectangle defined by the points (0,0) and (f1(xi), f2(xi)). An example for two-dimensional case is presented in Fig.4:

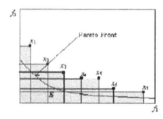

Figure 4: The metric S for the case of two objective functions and 7 decision vectors (x1, x2, ..., x7) for a minimization problem.

Annex B

Message-Passing Interface

MPI

MPI (Message-Passing Interface) is a message-passing library interface specification. Allparts of this definition are significant. MPI addresses primarily the message-passing parallelprogramming model, in which data is moved from the address space of one process to that of another process through cooperative operations on each process. (Extensions to the "classical" message-passing model are provided in collective operations, remote-memory access operations, dynamic process creation, and parallel I/O.)

MPI is a specification, not an implementation; there are multiple implementations of MPI. This specification is for a library interface; MPI is not a language, and all MPI operations are expressed as functions, subroutines, or methods, according to the appropriate language bindings, which for C, C++, Fortran-77, and Fortran-95, are part of the MPI standard. The standard has been defined through an open process by a community of parallel computing vendors, computer scientists, and application developers.

The main advantages of establishing a message-passing standard are portability and ease of use. In a distributed memory communication environment in which the higher level routines and/or abstractions are built upon lower level message-passing routines the benefits of standardization are particularly apparent. Furthermore, the definition of a message passing standard, such as that proposed here, provides vendors with a clearly defined base set of routines that they can implement efficiently, or in some cases provide hardware support for, thereby enhancing scalability.

The goal of the Message-Passing Interface simply stated is to develop a widely used standard for writing message-passing programs. As such the interface should establish a practical, portable, efficient, and flexible standard for message passing.

A complete list of goals follows.

• Design an application programming interface (not necessarily for compilers or a system implementation library).

• Allow efficient communication: Avoid memory-to-memory copying, allow overlap of computation and communication, and offload to communication co-processor, where available.

• Allow for implementations that can be used in a heterogeneous environment.

• Allow convenient C, C++, Fortran-77, and Fortran-95 bindings for the interface.

• Assume a reliable communication interface: the user need not cope with communication failures. Such failures are dealt with by the underlying communication subsystem.

• Define an interface that can be implemented on many vendor's platforms, with no significant changes in the underlying communication and system software.

• Semantics of the interface should be language independent.

• The interface should be designed to allow for thread safety.

Bibliography

[1]   M.Gzara, A.Essabri, T.Loukil-*Clustering based parallel multi-objective evolutionary algorithm with exploration exploitation Balance.*

[2] M.Gzara, A.Essabri, T.Loukil -*A Study of Distributed Evolutionary Algorithms for Multi-Objective Optimisation*

[3] E. Zitzler and L. Thiele. *An Evolutionary Approach for Multiobjective Optimization: The Strength Pareto Approach.* TIK Report 43, Computer Engineering and Networks Laboratory (TIK), ETH Zurich, May 1998.

[4] E. Zitzler, M. Laumanns, and L. Thiele. **SPEA2:** *Improving the Strength Pareto Evolutionary Algorithm.* TIK Report 103, Computer Engineering and Networks Laboratory (TIK), ETH Zurich, Zurich, Switzerland, 2001.

[5] E. Zitzler and L. Thiele. *Multiobjective Evolutionary Algorithms:*

Comparative Case Study and the Strength Pareto Approach. IEEE Transactions on Evolutionary Computation, November 1999.

[6] Srinivas, N. and K. Deb .*Multiobjective optimization using nondominated sorting in genetic algorithms.* In M. S. et al. (Ed.), *Parallel Problem Solving from Nature – PPSN VI*, Berlin, Springer. (2000).

[7] Deb, K., S. Agrawal, A. Pratap, and T. Meyarivan *A fast elitist nondominated sorting genetic algorithm for multi-objective optimization: NSGA-II.* In M. S. et al. (Ed.), *Parallel Problem Solving from Nature – PPSN VI*, Berlin, Springer. (2000).

[8] J⁻. Branke, H. Schmeck, K. Deb, M. Reddy.S .*Parallelizing Multi-Objective Evolutionary Algorithms: Cone Separation.* KanGAL Report Number 2004017.

[9] M. Laumanns, L. Thiele, and E. Zitzler. *An Efficient, Adaptive Parameter Variation Scheme for Metaheuristics Based on the Epsilon-Constraint Method. European Journal of Operational Research*, 169(3), March 2006.

[10]   G Lee Nelson.*An Application of Genetic Algorithms to the Growth and Development of Musical Organisms*.TIMARA Department Conservatory of Music Oberlin.

[11]   Carlos A. Coello Coello. **Basic Concepts** CINVESTAV-IPN Depto. de Ingenieria El'ectrica Seccion de Computacion .

[12]   **http://www.lifl.fr/OPAC/guimoo** user guide.

[13]   Brad L. Miller and David E.Golberg Genetic *algorithms, and the effect of Noise*. July   12,1995.

[14]   *G. Winter* [et al]. *Genetic algorithms in engineering and computer science.* c1995.

[15]   M.Obitko, *Introduction to genetic algorithm*.1998.

[16]   E. Zitzler - Evolutionary Algorithms for Multiobjective Optimization - In Evolutionary Methods for Design, Optimisation, and Control (EUROGEN 2001),. CIMNE, 2002.

[17] E. Zitzler, K. Deb, and L. Thiele. *Comparison of Multiobjective Evolutionary Algorithms: Empirical Results (Revised Version)*. TIK Report 70, Computer Engineering and Networks Laboratory (TIK), ETH Zurich, December 1999.

[18] Meunier, 2002

[19] Basseur et al., 2002

[20] Van Veldhuizen, 1999

[21] Zitzler, 1999

[22] E. Zitzler, M. Laumanns, and S. Bleuler. *A Tutorial on Evolutionary Multiobjective Optimization*. In X. Gandibleux et al., editors, *Metaheuristics for Multiobjective Optimisation*, volume 535 of *Lecture Notes in Economics and Mathematical Systems*. Springer, 2004.

[23]   M. Laumanns, L. Thiele, K. Deb, and E. Zitzler.-Archiving with Guaranteed Convergence And Diversity in Multi-objective Optimization-New York, NY, USA,

Morgan Kaufmann Publishers. In Genetic and Evolutionary Computation Conference
(GECCO 2002), July 2002.

[24] Silverman, B. W. (1986). *Density estimation for statistics and data analysis.*
London: Chapman and Hall.

[25] {zitzler,laumanns,thiele}@tik.ee.ethz.ch

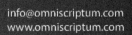